The Introvert's Guide to Balancing Life

The Introvert's Guide to Balancing Life

Monica Veronica

Copyright © 2024 by Monica Veronica
All rights reserved. No part of this book may be reproduced in any manner whatsoever without written permission except in the case of brief quotations embodied in critical articles and reviews.
First Printing, 2024

Contents

1 Understanding Introversion   1

2 Surviving a Busy Life as an Introvert   11

3 Time Management Strategies for Introverts   21

4 Finding Your Focus   31

5 Social Recharge Techniques for Introverts   41

6 Building a Supportive Network   49

7 Self-Care Practices for Introverts
59

8 Balancing Work and Personal Life
69

9	Thriving in Group Settings	79
10	Embracing Change and Growth	89
11	Conclusion: Your Journey as an Introvert	99

Understanding Introversion

The Nature of Introversion

Introversion is often misunderstood, yet it is a natural and valuable personality trait that shapes how many individuals interact with the world. At its core, introversion is characterized by a preference for solitary or small group activities, where introspection and deep thought thrive. Introverts typically find their energy from within, requiring moments of quiet reflection to recharge. Understanding the nature of introversion can help you embrace your unique qualities and navigate a busy life with confidence and grace.

As an introvert, you may find large social gatherings to be draining rather than invigorating. This is not a flaw but rather a reflection of your natural tendencies. While extroverts may thrive in social settings, introverts often prefer meaningful conversations over small talk and seek to connect on a deeper level. Recognizing the importance of these preferences allows you to structure your social interactions in a way that feels comfortable and fulfilling. Prioritizing quality over quantity can lead to more satisfying relationships and a sense of belonging without overwhelming your senses.

Time management can be particularly challenging for introverts in a fast-paced world. The constant demands of a busy life can lead to feelings of anxiety and overwhelm. To counteract this, consider implementing structured routines that include periods of solitude and reflection. By carving out time for yourself in your schedule, you create a sanctuary where you can recharge and regroup. This intentional approach not only helps you manage your responsibilities effectively but also honors your need for downtime, ultimately leading to greater productivity and creativity.

In the quest for balance, social recharge techniques become essential tools for introverts. These strategies can include engaging in solitary activities that you enjoy, such as reading, writing, or pursuing a hobby. Additionally, mindful practices like meditation or nature walks can provide the quiet space necessary to restore your energy. By developing a personal toolbox of recharge techniques, you empower yourself to navigate social obligations without depleting your reserves. Remember, it's perfectly acceptable to take a step back when you need to; honoring your boundaries is key to maintaining your well-being.

Embracing your introversion means recognizing that your unique perspective and approach to life are not only valid but valuable. The world needs the thoughtful insights and creativity that introverts bring to the table. By understanding the nature of your personality, you can develop strategies that align with your strengths. Celebrate your individuality and remember that finding balance is a journey. With the right tools and mindset, you can thrive in your busy life, cultivating both meaningful connections and the cherished solitude that fuels your spirit.

Common Misconceptions

Introverts often find themselves facing a myriad of misconceptions that can exacerbate the challenges of navigating a busy life. One common myth is that introverts are antisocial or dislike people. In reality, introverts thrive in social settings, but they may prefer smaller gatherings or meaningful one-on-one interactions. Understanding that introversion does not mean a lack of desire for connection can help introverts feel more empowered to seek out social opportunities that truly recharge them, rather than drain their energy.

Another prevalent misconception is that introverts are shy or socially awkward. While some introverts may indeed feel shy in certain situations, many are confident and articulate communicators when they are in comfortable environments. It's essential to recognize that introversion is simply a different way of processing social energy, not a deficiency. Embracing this understanding can lead to more authentic interactions and reduce the pressure to conform to extroverted norms, allowing introverts to shine in their unique way.

Time management is another area rife with misunderstandings. Many believe that introverts are less productive or unable to handle busy schedules. However, introverts often excel in environments that allow for deep focus and reflection. By leveraging their strengths, such as the ability to concentrate for extended periods, introverts can develop effective time management strategies that play to their preferences. This can include setting aside quiet blocks of time for work and ensuring regular intervals for recharging, which ultimately leads to greater productivity and satisfaction.

Additionally, some people think that introverts should simply "get over" their need for solitude and embrace a more extroverted lifestyle. This belief can be harmful, as it invalidates the introvert's need for downtime to process their experiences and recharge their energy. Instead of viewing solitude as a weakness, introverts should recognize it as a vital component of their well-being. By prioritizing self-care and scheduling time for reflection, introverts can cultivate a balanced life that honors their natural inclinations rather than forcing themselves into uncomfortable social situations.

Finally, there is a misconception that introverts must change who they are to succeed in a busy world. This notion can lead to feelings of inadequacy and overwhelm. Instead, introverts should focus on embracing their strengths and finding ways to navigate their environment in a way that feels authentic. By adopting strategies tailored to their unique needs, such as setting boundaries, creating supportive environments, and finding their ideal social rhythms, introverts can thrive in their personal and professional lives without compromising their true selves.

Embracing Your Introverted Self

Embracing your introverted self is a vital step toward achieving balance in a world that often celebrates extroverted traits. Introverts possess unique strengths that can be harnessed to navigate the complexities of daily life. By understanding and accepting your introverted nature, you can develop strategies that allow you to thrive in social situations while also honoring your need for solitude and reflection. Acknowledging your distinct qualities is not just an act of self-acceptance; it is a powerful tool that can enhance your overall well-being.

One of the core elements of embracing your introverted self is recognizing that your preferences are valid. While society may often push for loudness and constant connectivity, introverts bring depth and thoughtfulness to interactions. This perspective shift allows you to appreciate your own company and the benefits of solitude, which can lead to greater creativity and productivity. By celebrating the moments you spend alone, you can recharge your energy and cultivate a deeper understanding of your thoughts and feelings.

Effective time management is essential for introverts, especially when faced with the demands of a busy life. Prioritizing tasks and setting boundaries can help you maintain a sense of control over your schedule. Consider implementing techniques such as time blocking or the Pomodoro technique, allowing you to dedicate focused periods to work while ensuring you carve out time for breaks. By organizing your day in a way that respects your energy levels, you can minimize overwhelm and maximize your productivity, all while staying true to your introverted nature.

Social situations can often be draining for introverts, but learning to manage and recharge during these times is crucial. Developing social recharge techniques can help you navigate gatherings and networking events with confidence. Practice setting limits on your social commitments, and don't hesitate to take breaks when you feel your energy waning. Finding quiet corners or stepping outside for fresh air can provide the necessary reset to help you re-engage with your environment. Remember, it's perfectly acceptable to honor your need for space, and doing so will enable you to enjoy social interactions more fully.

Ultimately, embracing your introverted self is about recognizing the value you bring to the world. Your thoughtful insights and ability to listen deeply are gifts that can enhance your relationships and professional endeavors. By nurturing your introverted qualities and implementing effective strategies, you can create a fulfilling life that balances the demands of the outside world with the restorative power of your inner world. Embrace who you are; the world needs your unique perspective, and finding harmony between your introverted nature and the busyness of life is not just possible but profoundly rewarding.

2

Surviving a Busy Life as an Introvert

Identifying Overwhelm Triggers

Identifying overwhelm triggers is a crucial first step for introverts seeking to navigate a busy world while maintaining their well-being. As an introvert, it's natural to feel overwhelmed in environments that demand constant social interaction or high levels of stimulation. Recognizing the specific situations, people, or environments that lead to feelings of overwhelm can empower you to manage your energy more effectively. By tuning into your emotional and physical responses, you can create a clearer picture of your triggers and develop strategies to address them.

One common trigger for many introverts is excessive social interaction. Attending large gatherings or networking events can quickly drain your energy, leaving you feeling exhausted and disoriented. Pay attention to how you feel before, during, and after such events. Do you find yourself feeling anxious or fatigued? Understanding these feelings can help you acknowledge when you need to take a step back or set limits on your social commitments. It's perfectly acceptable to excuse yourself early from a gathering or to opt-out of an event if it feels too overwhelming.

Another potential trigger is the pressure to multitask or manage too many responsibilities at once. Introverts often thrive in environments where they can focus on one task at a time. If you notice that juggling multiple projects or balancing various obligations leaves you feeling frazzled, it may be time to reevaluate your workload.

Prioritizing tasks and setting realistic deadlines can help you regain control and reduce that sense of overwhelm. Remember, it's not a sign of weakness to ask for help or to delegate tasks when necessary.

Physical environments can also play a significant role in how you experience overwhelm. Crowded spaces, loud noises, or chaotic settings can be particularly unsettling for introverts. Take note of the environments that leave you feeling drained or overstimulated. Once you identify these spaces, you can seek alternatives that provide a calmer atmosphere. Whether it's finding a quiet café instead of a bustling restaurant or choosing a peaceful park for a break, small adjustments in your surroundings can make a significant difference in your overall comfort and energy levels.

Lastly, interpersonal dynamics can contribute to feelings of overwhelm. Certain relationships may require more emotional labor than others, leading to fatigue. Pay attention to how specific interactions affect your mood and energy. If you find certain individuals consistently drain you, it may be worth reassessing how much time you spend with them. Surround yourself with people who uplift and energize you, and don't hesitate to set boundaries where needed. By consciously identifying and addressing your overwhelm triggers, you can cultivate a more balanced and fulfilling life as an introvert, allowing you to thrive even in demanding situations.

Setting Personal Boundaries

Setting personal boundaries is essential for introverts navigating the demands of a busy life. As natural introspectors, introverts often find themselves overwhelmed by external expectations and social obligations. Establishing clear boundaries is not only a way to protect your energy but also a means to reclaim your time. By defining what you are comfortable with and what you need from yourself and others, you create a safe space that allows you to thrive without feeling drained.

One of the first steps in setting personal boundaries is self-awareness. Take the time to reflect on your limits; consider what situations or interactions leave you feeling exhausted or stressed. This introspection will empower you to identify areas in your life where boundaries are necessary. Whether it's declining invitations to social events or limiting your availability for work-related tasks, understanding your needs is crucial. Remember, recognizing your limits is a strength, not a weakness. It allows you to prioritize your well-being and focus on activities that invigorate you.

Communicating your boundaries can feel daunting, especially for those who prefer to avoid confrontation. However, it is possible to express your needs in a respectful and assertive manner. Practice framing your boundaries in positive terms, emphasizing your desire for balance rather than focusing on what you are saying no to. For example, instead of simply declining a social invitation, you might say, "I really appreciate the invite, but I need some quiet time to recharge." This approach not only respects your needs but also helps others understand and accept your boundaries.

Consistency is key when it comes to maintaining your boundaries. It can be tempting to bend your rules for the sake of others, but doing so often leads to resentment and burnout. Hold firm to your guidelines and remind yourself of the importance of your mental and emotional health. By being consistent, you reinforce your commitment to your well-being, making it easier for others to respect your limits. Over time, as you honor your own boundaries, you'll notice a greater sense of control over your life and a reduction in feelings of overwhelm.

Lastly, remember that setting personal boundaries is not a one-time event but an ongoing process. As your life evolves, so too will your needs and limits. Regularly revisit and adjust your boundaries as necessary to ensure they align with your current circumstances. Embrace the idea that it's perfectly acceptable to reevaluate your boundaries in response to changing situations. By doing so, you cultivate a nurturing environment that supports your introverted nature, allowing you to flourish amidst the demands of a busy life.

The Power of Saying No

The ability to say no is a crucial skill for introverts navigating a busy life. Introverts often find themselves overwhelmed by social obligations and external pressures, leading to burnout and exhaustion. Embracing the power of saying no allows you to prioritize your own needs and create a life that aligns with your values. Recognizing that your time and energy are finite resources is the first step toward reclaiming control over your schedule. By learning to assertively decline invitations and commitments that do not serve you, you can create space for activities that genuinely recharge your batteries.

Saying no can feel daunting, especially for those who are naturally inclined to please others. However, it is essential to remember that your needs are just as important as anyone else's. When you say yes to everything, you risk spreading yourself too thin, which can lead to feelings of resentment and frustration. By setting boundaries, you not only protect your well-being but also communicate to others that your time is valuable. This shift in mindset empowers you to approach your life with intention, ensuring that each commitment you make enhances rather than detracts from your overall quality of life.

In practice, saying no doesn't have to be confrontational or harsh. It can be conveyed with kindness and respect, allowing you to maintain your relationships while still prioritizing your own needs. Consider using phrases that express gratitude for the invitation or opportunity while clearly stating your inability to participate. This approach helps you remain true to your values without compromising your peace. Over time, as you practice saying no, you will find that it becomes easier and more natural, reducing the anxiety often associated with declining requests.

Additionally, saying no frees up valuable time and energy that you can redirect toward activities that nourish your introverted spirit. Whether it's spending quiet time at home, engaging in a favorite hobby, or simply resting, these moments are vital for your mental health and well-being. By consciously choosing how you spend your time, you create a balance that allows for social interactions when you feel ready and engaged, while also carving out time for solitude and reflection, which are essential for recharging.

Ultimately, embracing the power of saying no is an act of self-care that can transform your experience as an introvert in a busy world. It fosters a deeper understanding of your own limits and desires, leading to a more fulfilling life. By prioritizing your needs and practicing assertiveness, you cultivate a lifestyle that honors both your social connections and your need for solitude. Remember, saying no is not just a rejection; it is an affirmation of what truly matters to you, paving the way for a more balanced and authentic existence.

3

Time Management Strategies for Introverts

Prioritizing Tasks Effectively

Prioritizing tasks effectively can be a game-changer for introverts navigating the complexities of daily life. As an introvert, you may often find yourself overwhelmed by the demands of a busy schedule, leading to stress and exhaustion.

The key to overcoming this challenge lies in understanding which tasks are truly essential and aligning them with your personal values and energy levels. By taking the time to assess what matters most to you, you can create a roadmap that helps you focus on the right tasks while minimizing distractions and unnecessary commitments.

One effective approach to prioritization is the Eisenhower Matrix, a simple yet powerful tool that divides tasks into four categories: urgent and important, important but not urgent, urgent but not important, and neither urgent nor important. For introverts, this method allows you to clearly differentiate between what needs your immediate attention and what can wait. By categorizing your tasks, you can allocate your energy to those that align with your goals, enabling you to feel more in control and less overwhelmed by the demands of others.

Another helpful strategy is to implement the two-minute rule, which suggests that if a task can be completed in two minutes or less, do it immediately. This can be particularly beneficial for introverts, who may feel drained by the thought of accumulating small tasks. By quickly addressing minor responsibilities, such as responding to an email or organizing a workspace, you can prevent a backlog of tasks from building up and ensure that your mental space remains clear for more significant projects that require deeper focus and creativity.

In addition to these practical techniques, it's vital to honor your natural energy cycles. As an introvert, you may find that certain times of the day are more conducive to productivity than others. Schedule your most challenging tasks during peak energy hours, and reserve quieter times for less demanding activities. This tailored approach not only enhances your efficiency but also allows for necessary social recharge moments, where you can step back, reflect, and rejuvenate before diving into the next task.

Ultimately, prioritizing tasks effectively is about creating a balanced approach that respects your introverted nature while ensuring you stay on track. Embrace the power of saying no when necessary, allowing you to focus on what truly matters. By employing these strategies, you can navigate the complexities of a busy life with confidence and ease, transforming your experience from one of overwhelm to one of empowerment and fulfillment. Remember, it's perfectly okay to carve out your own path and prioritize your well-being in a world that often pushes for constant action.

Creating a Personalized Schedule

Creating a personalized schedule is an essential step for introverts seeking to navigate the complexities of a busy life while honoring their unique needs. Unlike extroverts, who may thrive on constant social interaction, introverts often require solitude and quiet time to recharge. By crafting a schedule tailored to your preferences, you can maintain a healthy balance between social obligations and personal downtime, ensuring you feel energized and engaged rather than overwhelmed.

Start by identifying your peak energy times throughout the day. Some introverts feel most alert and productive in the morning, while others may find their rhythm in the late afternoon or evening. By scheduling your most demanding tasks during these high-energy periods, you can maximize your efficiency and minimize stress. This approach allows you to tackle challenging work or social activities when you are naturally inclined to do so, freeing up the rest of your day for relaxation or lighter responsibilities.

It is crucial to incorporate breaks into your schedule, especially after social interactions or demanding tasks. These breaks can serve as vital recharge moments, allowing you to decompress and regain your energy. Consider scheduling short intervals of quiet time after meetings or social events, where you can engage in activities that you find soothing, such as reading, meditating, or taking a walk. Prioritizing these breaks not only helps you maintain your energy levels but also enhances your overall productivity and well-being.

Flexibility is another key component of a personalized schedule. Life can be unpredictable, and your needs may vary from day to day. Build in buffer times between commitments to accommodate unexpected changes or to simply allow yourself the grace to slow down when needed. By remaining adaptable, you can adjust your plans as necessary without feeling guilty or overwhelmed. This flexibility empowers you to create a rhythm that aligns with your introverted nature, making it easier to engage in social situations when they arise.

Lastly, remember that your schedule is a tool for your well-being, not a rigid set of rules. Embrace the process of trial and error as you figure out what works best for you. As you refine your schedule, listen to your instincts and adjust accordingly. Celebrate the small victories along the way and acknowledge the progress you make in finding a balance that honors both your social needs and your desire for solitude. By creating a personalized schedule that reflects your unique introverted nature, you can navigate the demands of life with confidence and ease.

Utilizing Time Blocks

Utilizing time blocks can be a game changer for introverts striving to navigate a busy life. By dedicating specific time periods to focused activities, you create a structure that allows you to manage your energy levels and commitments more effectively. This approach helps alleviate the overwhelm that often comes with a packed schedule, allowing you to carve out moments of solitude and reflection amidst the chaos. Embracing time blocks means you can honor your needs as an introvert while still making progress in your professional and personal life.

To begin implementing time blocks, start by assessing your daily and weekly commitments. Identify when you feel most energized and when your energy tends to dip. This knowledge will guide you in allocating your time wisely. For instance, you might find that your most productive hours are in the morning when you can tackle challenging tasks without distractions. By designating this time for deep work, you can maximize your output while reserving the afternoons for lighter, less demanding tasks or social interactions.

Once you have your time blocks set, it's important to protect them fiercely. This means communicating your schedule to others and setting boundaries around your availability. As an introvert, it's essential to guard your personal time to recharge. Let colleagues or family members know when you are unavailable, and encourage them to respect those boundaries. By doing so, you cultivate an environment that honors your need for quiet and reflection, ultimately leading to greater productivity and satisfaction.

Incorporating breaks within your time blocks is equally vital. Introverts often require moments of solitude to recharge, especially after engaging in social activities or intense work sessions. Schedule short breaks between your blocks to step away, breathe, or enjoy a calming activity like reading or journaling. These intervals not only restore your energy but also enhance your focus when you return to your tasks. By allowing yourself these necessary pauses, you can maintain a balanced approach to productivity without feeling drained.

Lastly, reflect on your time-blocking experience regularly. Assess what works and what doesn't, adjusting your blocks as needed. This adaptable mindset ensures that your time management strategy evolves with your changing needs and circumstances. Embrace the process, and remember that finding balance is a journey. By utilizing time blocks, you empower yourself to navigate a busy life with intention, allowing your introverted nature to thrive amidst the demands of the world.

4

Finding Your Focus

Minimizing Distractions

In a world that often feels overwhelmingly loud and bustling, introverts frequently find themselves struggling to carve out moments of peace. Minimizing distractions is a crucial step in reclaiming your time and energy. By creating environments that nurture your need for quiet, you can foster productivity and mental clarity. Begin by assessing your surroundings—both physical and digital. Identify the noise and interruptions that drain your focus. Whether it's a cluttered workspace, constant notifications, or even the chatter of nearby colleagues, acknowledging these distractions is the first step toward managing them effectively.

Once you have pinpointed the sources of distraction, take actionable steps to mitigate them. For your physical space, consider adopting a minimalist approach. Keep only essential items on your desk, and use organizers to create a clean and inviting environment. If your home or work area is prone to noise, invest in noise-canceling headphones or soft background music that can help drown out disruptive sounds. In the digital realm, turn off non-essential notifications on your devices and schedule specific times to check emails or messages. By controlling your environment, you empower yourself to focus and recharge without the constant pull of distractions.

Time management is another essential tool in your arsenal. As an introvert, it's vital to structure your day in a way that honors your natural rhythms. Block out periods of uninterrupted work time, interspersed with breaks that allow for recharging. Use techniques like the Pomodoro Technique, where you work for 25 minutes and then take a 5-minute break. This not only helps maintain focus but also provides regular intervals for mental rest. Remember, your energy levels are finite, and managing your time wisely can dramatically reduce the feeling of being overwhelmed.

Social interactions can also be a source of distraction, particularly for introverts who may find large gatherings draining. To minimize this impact, consider setting boundaries around your social engagements. Prioritize quality over quantity; choose smaller gatherings where meaningful conversations can flourish. Be honest with friends and family about your need for solitude, and don't hesitate to decline invitations that feel too taxing. Developing a repertoire of polite but firm responses can help you maintain your social life without overextending yourself.

Lastly, incorporate techniques for social recharge into your routine. After a busy day or week filled with interactions, carve out time for activities that replenish your energy. Whether it's reading a book, taking a nature walk, or practicing a hobby you love, these moments of quiet reflection are essential for your well-being. Cultivating a lifestyle that honors your introverted nature will not only enhance your productivity but also bring a sense of balance and fulfillment to your life. Embrace the power of minimizing distractions, and watch as you flourish amidst the chaos.

Techniques for Deep Work

Deep work is a valuable skill for introverts, allowing them to harness their inner strengths and focus intensely on tasks that require high levels of concentration. One effective technique for achieving deep work is the Pomodoro Technique, which involves working in focused sprints of 25 minutes followed by a 5-minute break. This method not only helps maintain high levels of productivity but also allows introverts to recharge briefly before diving back into their tasks. By structuring work periods and breaks, introverts can manage their energy levels effectively, making it easier to stay engaged and productive throughout the day.

Another powerful technique is time blocking, which involves dedicating specific chunks of time to particular tasks or projects. For introverts, this method provides a sense of control over their schedule and allows them to create a work environment that minimizes distractions. By allocating uninterrupted blocks of time for deep work, introverts can immerse themselves in their tasks without the constant pull of notifications or social obligations. Additionally, planning for these blocks in advance can help reduce anxiety and create a more predictable routine, giving introverts the confidence to tackle even the most challenging projects.

Creating an optimal environment for deep work is essential for introverts. This might involve setting up a dedicated workspace that is free from distractions, such as noise or clutter. Some introverts find solace in using noise-canceling headphones or playing soft background music to help them focus. Others may benefit from incorporating elements of nature, like plants or natural light, to enhance their sense of calm and concentration. Tailoring the workspace to individual preferences can make a significant difference in how effectively deep work is performed, allowing introverts to thrive in their personal and professional lives.

Mindfulness techniques can also play a crucial role in facilitating deep work for introverts. Practicing mindfulness helps to clear the mind of distractions and fosters a sense of presence that is essential for focused work. Simple exercises, such as deep breathing or short meditation sessions, can ground introverts and prepare them for their deep work sessions. By integrating mindfulness into their routines, introverts can enhance their ability to concentrate and achieve a flow state, where they feel fully immersed in their tasks and less overwhelmed by external demands.

Finally, establishing boundaries is vital for maintaining deep work in the busy lives of introverts. Communicating needs to colleagues, friends, and family can help create a supportive environment where uninterrupted work time is respected. This might mean scheduling specific "do not disturb" periods or letting others know when you are unavailable for social interactions. By setting these boundaries, introverts can protect their time and energy, allowing them to engage in deep work without the constant pressure of social obligations. Embracing these techniques empowers introverts to navigate their busy lives with confidence and balance, leading to greater satisfaction and success.

The Importance of Breaks

In the fast-paced world we inhabit, the importance of taking breaks cannot be overstated, especially for introverts. Unlike extroverts who may thrive in constant social interaction, introverts often find that prolonged engagement can lead to exhaustion. Breaks are not just a luxury; they are essential for recharging our mental and emotional batteries. By recognizing the necessity of these pauses, introverts can navigate their busy lives with greater ease and effectiveness.

Breaks offer introverts the opportunity to step back and assess their surroundings. This reflection time is crucial for processing experiences and emotions, enabling us to return to our tasks with renewed clarity and focus. Whether it's a short walk outside, a few moments of deep breathing, or simply enjoying a quiet cup of tea, these breaks help create a buffer against the chaos of daily life. Embracing this downtime allows introverts to regroup and strategize, transforming overwhelming situations into manageable ones.

Furthermore, breaks can significantly enhance time management for introverts. By scheduling intentional pauses throughout the day, introverts can prevent burnout and maintain a steady workflow. Instead of pushing through fatigue, taking a short break can lead to increased productivity. This approach not only maximizes efficiency but also helps introverts feel more in control of their time. When we honor our need for breaks, we cultivate a healthier relationship with our responsibilities, reducing stress and preventing overwhelm.

Social recharge techniques are equally vital in understanding the importance of breaks. Introverts thrive in solitude, and incorporating breaks into social activities can make interactions feel less draining. Planning for moments of quiet during larger gatherings or setting boundaries around social commitments allows introverts to engage without feeling depleted. These strategies empower us to participate in social events while maintaining our well-being, ensuring that we can enjoy the company of others without sacrificing our energy.

Ultimately, recognizing the importance of breaks is about honoring our unique needs as introverts. By prioritizing these moments of respite, we can create a balanced life that accommodates our introspective nature. Breaks are not signs of weakness; they are tools for resilience. Embracing this perspective allows introverts to thrive in a busy world, transforming the way we approach our daily lives and interactions. Remember, taking a step back is often the first step toward moving forward with confidence and clarity.

5

Social Recharge Techniques for Introverts

Recognizing Your Social Battery Levels

Recognizing your social battery levels is essential for maintaining balance in a busy life as an introvert. Just as our electronic devices require regular charging to function effectively, so do we. Social interactions, while crucial for personal and professional growth, can drain an introvert's energy more quickly than for others. Understanding where you stand on the spectrum of social energy can empower you to make informed decisions about when to engage and when to retreat for recharging.

Begin by tuning into your feelings during and after social interactions. Pay attention to physical cues such as fatigue, irritability, or a sense of overwhelm. These signs can indicate that your social battery is running low. Additionally, consider your emotional responses; if you find yourself feeling drained or needing extended alone time after a gathering, it's a clear signal that your social energy has been depleted. By acknowledging these feelings, you can better navigate your social calendar, ensuring that you don't overcommit and allowing yourself the necessary time to recharge.

Tracking your social interactions can also be a helpful strategy. Keeping a simple log of your activities can reveal patterns in your energy levels. Note when you feel most energized and when you feel the need to withdraw. This practice can provide valuable insight into how different environments and social settings impact your energy. Over time, you'll develop a clearer sense of what types of gatherings invigorate you and which ones leave you feeling drained. With this knowledge, you can make more conscious choices about your social engagements.

Another vital aspect is understanding your unique recharge needs. Just as we all have varied social preferences, our methods of recharging differ too. Some introverts may find solitude to be the most effective way to regain energy, while others may prefer engaging in low-key activities with a close friend. Experiment with different recharge techniques, whether it's reading a book, taking a nature walk, or practicing mindfulness. By discovering what works best for you, you can create a personalized strategy that aligns with your needs.

Ultimately, recognizing your social battery levels allows you to embrace your introverted nature without guilt or pressure. It empowers you to navigate social situations in a way that honors your energy and fosters genuine connections. By prioritizing your well-being and understanding your limits, you can thrive in a busy life, turning what may seem like a challenge into an opportunity for growth and self-discovery. Remember, it's perfectly okay to say no or take a step back; doing so is not a sign of weakness but rather a testament to your self-awareness and commitment to maintaining your balance.

Planning for Social Events

Planning social events as an introvert can feel daunting, but with the right strategies, it can also be a rewarding experience. The key is to approach the planning process with a clear vision of what you want and a focus on your comfort. Start by selecting the type of event that resonates with you. Whether it's a small gathering with close friends or a larger celebration, knowing your preferences will help guide decisions that align with your energy levels and social needs.

Next, consider the logistics of your event. Choose a location that feels safe and comfortable for you. This could be your home, a quiet café, or a serene outdoor space. Think about the time of day as well; hosting an event in the afternoon might allow for a more relaxed atmosphere compared to a late-night gathering. Keep in mind that the environment can significantly impact your energy, so opt for settings that foster ease and enjoyment.

When it comes to inviting guests, be selective. You don't have to invite everyone you know; instead, focus on those who uplift you and whom you genuinely want to spend time with. Personalize your invitations to create a sense of connection and warmth. This approach not only eases your mind about the social demands but also ensures that you will engage with people who make you feel comfortable and understood.

As the event approaches, take time for self-care. Prepare in a way that feels manageable, whether that means making a detailed checklist or keeping it simple. On the day of the event, allow yourself moments to recharge. Set up a cozy corner where you can take short breaks if needed. Acknowledging your limits and planning for downtime will help you enjoy the event without feeling overwhelmed.

Finally, after the event, reflect on your experience. Celebrate the moments that brought you joy and acknowledge any challenges you faced. This reflection not only helps you appreciate your efforts but also provides insights for future events. Each social gathering is an opportunity to learn more about your preferences and boundaries, allowing you to create a balanced social life that honors your introverted nature while still embracing connection.

Creating a Recharge Routine

Creating a recharge routine is essential for introverts navigating the demands of a busy life. While the world often celebrates the extroverted approach to socializing and productivity, introverts thrive when they allow themselves the space and time to recharge. A well-crafted routine can serve as a sanctuary, helping you to regain your energy, focus, and enthusiasm for the tasks and interactions that lie ahead. By prioritizing your needs, you can cultivate a balanced lifestyle that honors both your introverted nature and the realities of a fast-paced environment.

To begin designing your recharge routine, start by identifying the activities that genuinely refresh you. These might include quiet hobbies like reading, journaling, or engaging in creative pursuits like painting or crafting. Alternatively,

THE INTROVERT'S GUIDE TO BALANCING LIFE

you may find solace in nature through walking, hiking, or simply spending time in a garden. The key is to recognize what makes you feel grounded and rejuvenated. Consider keeping a journal where you can jot down your feelings after various activities, helping you pinpoint what truly nourishes your spirit.

Next, establish a dedicated time each day or week for your recharge activities. Consistency is crucial; by carving out intentional time for yourself, you signal to your mind and body that your needs are important. This could be as simple as reserving an hour each evening after work to unwind with a good book or planning a quiet weekend morning for reflection and self-care. Block this time on your calendar, treat it as an appointment, and guard it fiercely against interruptions. This commitment will reinforce the importance of self-care in your life.

As you incorporate your recharge routine, consider integrating mindfulness practices to enhance your experience. Mindfulness techniques, such as meditation or deep-breathing exercises, can help quiet the noise of everyday stressors and draw your focus inward. Even a few minutes of focused breathing can help clear your mind and recharge your emotional batteries. By being present in these moments, you create a deeper connection to your chosen activities, allowing for a more profound rejuvenation that can carry you through the busyness of life.

Finally, remain flexible and open to adjusting your routine as needed. Life can be unpredictable, and what works one week may not resonate the next. Periodically reassess your recharge activities and their effectiveness. If you find yourself feeling drained, it might be a sign to explore new hobbies or change your environment. Embrace the journey of self-discovery, and remember that prioritizing your well-being is not only essential for you but also enriches your interactions with others. By creating and nurturing a recharge routine, you empower yourself to thrive in a busy world while embracing the beauty of your introverted nature.

Building a Supportive Network

Connecting with Like-Minded Individuals

Connecting with like-minded individuals can be a transformative experience for introverts navigating a busy life. While social interactions can sometimes feel overwhelming, finding people who share similar values and interests creates a comfortable space where meaningful connections can flourish. This sense of community not only alleviates feelings of isolation but also reinforces the idea that introverts can thrive in social settings, provided they are surrounded by understanding and supportive individuals.

One of the best strategies for introverts seeking to connect with others is to identify environments that cater to their interests. Joining clubs, attending workshops, or participating in online forums related to hobbies or professional development can facilitate organic interactions with individuals who resonate with one's passions. These settings often foster deeper conversations that go beyond small talk, allowing introverts to engage in discussions that ignite their enthusiasm and creativity. By focusing on shared interests, the pressure to perform socially diminishes, making it easier to forge authentic connections.

In addition to pursuing interest-based gatherings, leveraging technology can significantly enhance an introvert's ability to connect with others. Online platforms and social media offer a unique opportunity to engage with like-minded individuals from the comfort of home. Virtual meetups, webinars, and online communities provide a space for introverts to express their thoughts and ideas without the immediate pressure of in-person interactions. This can serve as a stepping stone to face-to-face connections, as relationships built online often transition smoothly into the real world when both parties feel ready.

It is also essential for introverts to practice self-compassion while navigating social interactions. The journey to forming connections is not always linear, and it is perfectly normal to feel drained or overwhelmed at times. Embracing the idea that socializing is a skill that can be developed over time encourages patience and understanding towards oneself. By acknowledging personal limits and honoring the need for solitude when necessary, introverts can recharge effectively, allowing them to return to social situations with renewed energy and enthusiasm.

Ultimately, connecting with like-minded individuals is about creating a supportive network that fosters growth and understanding. By engaging in environments that align with personal interests, utilizing technology for outreach, and practicing self-compassion, introverts can build fulfilling relationships that enrich their lives.

These connections not only provide a sense of belonging but also contribute to a balanced approach to life, allowing introverts to navigate the busy world with confidence and grace.

Nurturing Meaningful Relationships

Nurturing meaningful relationships as an introvert can feel like a daunting task, especially in a world that often prioritizes extroverted qualities. However, cultivating deep connections is not only possible, but it can also be incredibly rewarding. By embracing your natural strengths and adopting a few strategic approaches, you can build relationships that nourish your spirit and enhance your overall well-being.

To start, it's essential to recognize that quality often trumps quantity in relationships. Introverts tend to thrive in smaller, more intimate settings where genuine conversations can flourish. Focus on nurturing a few key relationships rather than spreading yourself too thin. Invest time in getting to know individuals who resonate with your values and interests. These deeper connections can provide the emotional support and understanding that introverts often seek, making the effort worthwhile.

Creating opportunities for connection can also be tailored to your preferences. Consider organizing small gatherings or one-on-one outings that align with your comfort level. Engaging in activities that you genuinely enjoy can naturally lead to bonding experiences. Whether it's a book club, a hiking trip, or a cozy coffee date, these settings allow for meaningful interactions without the overwhelming pressure of larger social events. Remember that you have the power to shape your social experiences in a way that feels authentic to you.

Effective communication is another crucial component of nurturing relationships. As an introvert, you may prefer to express your thoughts and feelings in writing rather than through spontaneous conversation. Don't hesitate to use this strength to your advantage. Sending thoughtful messages, sharing articles, or even writing letters can help you articulate your feelings and maintain connections. This approach not only deepens your relationships but also allows you to engage on your own terms, making social interactions feel less taxing.

Finally, prioritize self-care and social recharge techniques to maintain your energy levels. Building meaningful relationships requires emotional investment, and it's essential to replenish your reserves. Schedule regular downtime after social interactions to reflect and recharge, whether that means spending time alone with a good book or engaging in a favorite hobby. By honoring your need for solitude, you can approach your relationships with renewed enthusiasm and an open heart, ultimately fostering connections that enrich your life.

Seeking Out Introvert-Friendly Spaces

Finding environments that cater to introverts can be a transformative experience, allowing you to thrive in a world that often feels overwhelming. Introvert-friendly spaces are those where you can recharge, focus, and engage in meaningful interactions without the drain of excessive stimulation. Whether it's a cozy coffee shop, a quiet library, or a serene park, these spaces can provide the refuge you need to maintain your well-being amidst the chaos of daily life. By intentionally seeking out these environments, you can create a supportive backdrop for your personal and professional growth.

When searching for introvert-friendly spaces, consider locations that prioritize calmness and solitude. Look for establishments that offer comfortable seating arrangements, soft lighting, and minimal distractions. Public libraries are an excellent option, as they not only provide a quiet atmosphere but also offer resources for personal development. Cafés with a relaxed vibe can serve as a great alternative, especially those that are less crowded during off-peak hours. Taking the time to identify these spaces can significantly enhance your ability to concentrate and recharge.

In addition to traditional locations, many introverts find solace in nature. Parks, gardens, and nature trails provide a peaceful retreat from the hustle and bustle of urban life. These environments encourage mindfulness and reflection, allowing you to connect with yourself and the world around you. Spending time outdoors can also help to reduce stress and improve your mood, making it an ideal way to recharge your energy levels. Make it a habit to explore local green spaces and discover the tranquility they offer.

Creating introvert-friendly spaces in your home is just as important as finding them outside. Designate a specific area in your living space where you can retreat when you need to unwind. This could be a reading nook, a meditation corner, or simply a comfortable chair where you can enjoy your favorite activities in peace. Personalizing this space with elements that bring you joy—such as books, plants, or calming colors—can make a significant difference in how you feel when you need to recharge. Your home should be a sanctuary that supports your needs as an introvert.

Finally, don't hesitate to communicate your needs to friends, family, and colleagues. Sharing your preference for introvert-friendly environments can help others understand your boundaries and support you in creating these spaces. Whether it's suggesting quieter venues for gatherings or advocating for a more balanced approach to social events, open communication can foster understanding and respect for your introverted nature. By surrounding yourself with people who appreciate and acknowledge your needs, you can create a harmonious balance between social obligations and personal recharge time.

Self-Care Practices for Introverts

The Importance of Solitude

Solitude is not merely the absence of others; it is a state of being that allows introverts to reconnect with themselves, recharge their energy, and cultivate their inner thoughts. In a world that often celebrates busyness and social interactions, it is essential for introverts to recognize the value of solitude. Embracing moments of quiet can lead to profound self-discovery and creativity, enabling introverts to thrive amidst the chaos of daily life. By understanding the importance of solitude, introverts can create a sanctuary where their minds can wander freely and their spirits can rejuvenate.

In solitude, introverts find the space to reflect on their experiences and thoughts. This reflection is crucial for personal growth and emotional well-being. It allows them to process their feelings, analyze their interactions, and gain clarity about their goals and desires. By taking the time to be alone, introverts can sift through the noise of everyday life and emerge with a clearer understanding of who they are and what they want. This self-awareness is a powerful tool that can enhance their decision-making skills and lead to more fulfilling relationships and experiences.

Moreover, solitude serves as a fertile ground for creativity. Many introverts are natural thinkers and problem solvers who thrive when given the opportunity to explore their ideas without interruption. In the quiet of their own company, they can brainstorm, write, or engage in artistic endeavors without the pressure of external judgment. Encouraging regular periods of solitude can unleash a torrent of creativity and innovation, allowing introverts to express themselves in ways that resonate deeply with their authentic selves. This creative outlet is not only fulfilling but also serves as a vital form of self-care.

Time management strategies for introverts often involve carving out intentional periods of solitude within their busy schedules. By prioritizing alone time, introverts can prevent feelings of overwhelm and burnout. Simple practices such as setting aside an hour each day for personal reflection, engaging in a favorite hobby, or going for a quiet walk can significantly impact their overall well-being. These moments of solitude are not just breaks from social obligations; they are essential components of a balanced life that help introverts maintain their energy levels and focus throughout the day.

Finally, embracing solitude can enhance social recharge techniques for introverts. When they allow themselves the necessary time to decompress alone, they equip themselves with the emotional resources needed for social interactions.

This recharge period can make social gatherings feel more manageable and enjoyable, rather than draining. By recognizing solitude as an essential aspect of their lifestyle, introverts can develop a sustainable approach to balancing their social and personal needs. In doing so, they can navigate the complexities of life with greater ease, confidence, and joy.

Mindfulness and Meditation

Mindfulness and meditation serve as powerful tools for introverts navigating the complexities of a busy life. Embracing these practices can create a sanctuary where you can retreat from the chaos of daily demands. For many introverts, the world often feels overwhelming, filled with social obligations and noise that can drain energy. Mindfulness, the practice of being present in the moment, allows you to step back and find calm amidst the storm. It encourages a deeper connection with your thoughts and feelings, fostering a sense of peace that is essential for maintaining balance.

Meditation complements mindfulness by offering a structured way to cultivate inner stillness. Even a few minutes spent in meditation can provide a refreshing reset, making it easier to manage stress and anxiety. For introverts, this quiet time is not just a luxury; it is a necessity. Setting aside time each day for meditation can enhance your focus, improve your emotional regulation, and increase your overall well-being. You may find that after a brief session of deep breathing or guided imagery, you emerge feeling rejuvenated, ready to tackle whatever the day brings.

Incorporating mindfulness into daily activities can also be an accessible way for introverts to practice this vital skill. Whether it's savoring your morning cup of tea or taking a mindful walk in nature, these moments of awareness can enrich your day. Engaging fully in activities allows you to cultivate a sense of gratitude and presence, reducing feelings of overwhelm. By intentionally slowing down and observing your surroundings, you can create pockets of peace that counterbalance the busyness of life.

Social recharge techniques can be enhanced through mindfulness and meditation. Introverts often need time to recover after social interactions, and using mindfulness techniques can help facilitate this process. Consider using deep breathing exercises or visualizations to center yourself after a gathering. By acknowledging your need for solitude and employing mindfulness practices, you can transform downtime into a restorative experience. This proactive approach not only aids in social recovery but also reinforces the importance of self-care in your routine.

Ultimately, integrating mindfulness and meditation into your life is about finding what works best for you. Start small, perhaps with a few minutes of focused breathing each day, and gradually build on your practice. Over time, you may notice significant shifts in how you handle stress and engage with the world around you. Embrace these moments of stillness as opportunities for growth and self-discovery. By prioritizing mindfulness and meditation, you empower yourself to thrive in a busy life, ensuring that your introverted spirit remains vibrant and balanced.

Engaging in Creative Outlets

Engaging in creative outlets can be a transformative experience for introverts, providing a much-needed escape from the busyness of everyday life. In a world that often feels overwhelming, tapping into your creative side can serve as a sanctuary where you can recharge and reconnect with your inner self. Whether through writing, painting, crafting, or any other form of expression, these activities allow you to channel your thoughts and emotions into something tangible. This not only fosters self-discovery but also enhances your well-being, making it easier to navigate the demands of a hectic lifestyle.

For many introverts, creative pursuits can be particularly appealing due to their inherently personal nature. Unlike social engagements that may drain your energy, creative outlets provide a safe space where you can express yourself on your own terms. You can choose to create in solitude, allowing your thoughts to flow freely without the pressure of external expectations. This process can rejuvenate your spirit, offering a refreshing break from the constant stimulation of the outside world. Embracing creativity allows you to set boundaries and prioritize your needs, giving you the power to reclaim your time and energy.

Time management is crucial for introverts striving to balance their busy lives, and incorporating creative activities into your routine can be a game-changer. By scheduling specific times for creative expression, you can ensure that you have dedicated moments to unwind and explore your passions. Consider setting aside even a small portion of your day for these activities, whether it's a few minutes of journaling in the morning or an hour of painting in the evening. This not only helps you stay organized but also creates a sense of anticipation for these moments of joy, enriching your daily experience.

Additionally, engaging in creative outlets can serve as a powerful tool for social recharge. While social interactions can often be draining, creative activities provide a different avenue for connection. Joining a local art class, writing group, or craft circle allows you to meet like-minded individuals in a relaxed environment. These gatherings often foster a sense of camaraderie that is less about small talk and more about shared passions. By participating in such activities, you can cultivate relationships that honor your introverted nature while still providing the social engagement that can be invigorating.

Ultimately, embracing creativity can lead to a more balanced and fulfilling life as an introvert. It is a reminder that you can thrive in your own way, creating space for both solitude and connection. By prioritizing creative outlets, you not only enrich your life but also develop resilience against the stresses of a busy schedule. As you explore your creative side, remember to be gentle with yourself and allow for exploration without judgment. This journey is uniquely yours, and each step taken in creative expression is a step toward greater balance and harmony in your life.

8

Balancing Work and Personal Life

Remote Work Benefits and Challenges

Remote work has transformed the professional landscape, offering a unique set of benefits that can be particularly advantageous for introverts. One of the most significant advantages is the ability to create a personalized work environment. Introverts often thrive in spaces that reflect their preferences, allowing them to control noise levels, lighting, and overall ambiance. This autonomy can lead to increased productivity and comfort, enabling introverts to perform at their best without the distractions commonly found in traditional office settings.

Additionally, remote work provides flexibility that can be a game-changer for introverts managing their time and energy. The ability to set one's hours according to personal peak productivity times means that introverts can work when they feel most focused, whether that's early in the morning or late at night. This flexibility allows for better integration of work and personal life, reducing the stress of commuting and enabling introverts to allocate time for recharging activities, such as reading, walking, or engaging in hobbies that nurture their well-being.

Despite these benefits, remote work also presents challenges that introverts may need to navigate. The lack of in-person social interaction can lead to feelings of isolation, which can be particularly difficult for those who recharge through solitude yet still crave some connection. To counter this, introverts can leverage technology to maintain relationships with colleagues through virtual coffee breaks or online team-building activities. These interactions can foster a sense of community while allowing introverts to manage their energy levels by participating on their own terms.

Another challenge of remote work is the potential for blurred boundaries between personal and professional life. Introverts may find it tempting to overcommit to work tasks, leading to burnout. It is crucial for introverts to establish firm boundaries and dedicated workspaces to create a clear distinction between work and personal time. Implementing time management strategies, such as the Pomodoro technique or scheduled breaks, can help maintain productivity while ensuring that there is ample time for recharging and self-care.

Ultimately, embracing remote work as an introvert requires a balance of taking advantage of its benefits while proactively addressing its challenges. By creating a tailored workspace, utilizing flexible scheduling, maintaining social connections, and setting boundaries, introverts can thrive in a remote work environment. This journey not only enhances professional satisfaction but also supports personal growth, allowing introverts to navigate their busy lives with confidence and resilience.

Establishing Work-Life Boundaries

Establishing work-life boundaries is essential for introverts who often find themselves overwhelmed by the demands of a busy life. As an introvert, you may thrive in solitude and need time to recharge after social interactions. By clearly defining the boundaries between your work and personal life, you can create a sanctuary that allows you to rejuvenate and maintain your well-being. It's crucial to recognize that these boundaries are not just about saying no to others but also about saying yes to yourself and your needs.

One effective strategy for establishing work-life boundaries is to set specific working hours. Choose a start and end time that accommodates your productivity peaks while also allowing for ample downtime. Communicate these hours to your colleagues and supervisors, ensuring they understand when you are available and when you are not. This practice helps create an environment where your time is respected, and it allows you to focus on your tasks without the constant pressure of being "on" at all hours. Remember, setting these boundaries is a form of self-care that can lead to greater productivity and satisfaction in your work.

Another important aspect is creating a physical workspace that signals when you are in "work mode" versus "personal time." Whether it's a dedicated home office, a specific corner of your living space, or simply a particular chair, having a defined area for work helps reinforce your boundaries. When you're in your designated workspace, you can immerse yourself in your tasks, knowing that once you step away, you are free to enjoy your personal time. This separation is vital for introverts, as it allows you to shift your mindset and recharge after a focused work session.

In addition to physical boundaries, consider incorporating technology to help manage your time effectively. Use tools like calendar apps or task management software to schedule breaks and downtime. By blocking out time for relaxation or personal hobbies, you are actively prioritizing your need for solitude and self-care. These digital aids can serve as reminders that your well-being is just as important as your work responsibilities. Embrace the flexibility these tools provide, and don't hesitate to adjust your schedule to better suit your introverted nature.

Lastly, be intentional about your social engagements and commitments outside of work. It's easy to overextend yourself, especially if you feel pressured to participate in every social event or obligation. Learn to assess your energy levels and say no when necessary. By curating your social calendar, you can ensure that you have ample time for recharging, allowing you to engage more fully in the activities you do choose to attend. Establishing these boundaries will not only preserve your energy but also enhance the quality of your interactions, making them more meaningful and enjoyable.

Prioritizing Personal Time

In the fast-paced world we live in, prioritizing personal time can feel like an impossible task, especially for introverts who often find social interactions draining. It's essential to recognize that personal time is not merely a luxury; it is a necessity for maintaining mental and emotional well-being. By carving out intentional moments for solitude and reflection, introverts can recharge their energy and better navigate the demands of daily life. Emphasizing the importance of self-care is the first step toward reclaiming your time and ensuring that it serves your needs.

Establishing boundaries around your personal time is crucial. This means learning to say no without guilt and recognizing that your energy is finite. Develop a clear understanding of your priorities and communicate them to those around you. When you make it known that personal time is a priority, it sets a precedent that others will respect. This will not only free you from overcommitment but also create a supportive environment where you can thrive. Remember, you are not being selfish; you are investing in your own well-being, which ultimately benefits everyone in your life.

Creating a schedule that reflects your needs can significantly enhance your ability to manage time effectively. Consider blocking out specific periods in your calendar solely for personal activities that recharge you. Whether it's reading a book, meditating, or simply enjoying a quiet cup of tea, these moments are vital for restoring your energy levels. Experiment with different time slots to find when you feel most rejuvenated and incorporate these into your weekly routine. By making personal time a non-negotiable part of your schedule, you send a clear message to yourself and others about its importance.

In addition to scheduling, it's helpful to adopt social recharge techniques. Think of these as small practices that can help you regain your energy without feeling overwhelmed. For instance, after a busy day of social interactions, consider engaging in a brief solo activity that brings you joy. This could be taking a walk in nature, journaling, or indulging in a favorite hobby. These practices don't have to be time-consuming; even a few minutes of solitude can make a significant difference in your energy levels. By intentionally integrating these recharge techniques into your life, you can maintain a balance between social obligations and personal time.

Lastly, remember that prioritizing personal time is not a one-time effort but an ongoing commitment. Life will always present new challenges and demands, so be prepared to reassess and adjust your boundaries and schedules as needed. Celebrate your progress and recognize the positive impact that personal time has on your overall well-being. By being proactive in prioritizing your needs, you empower yourself to navigate the complexities of life as an introvert, ultimately leading to a more fulfilling and balanced existence. Embrace this journey and know that you are taking essential steps toward a healthier, more energized you.

9

Thriving in Group Settings

Strategies for Navigating Social Gatherings

Social gatherings can often feel overwhelming for introverts, but with the right strategies, these events can become manageable and even enjoyable. One effective approach is to set clear intentions before attending a gathering. Consider what you hope to achieve, whether it's connecting with a specific person, enjoying a conversation, or simply practicing social skills. By having a clear purpose, you can navigate the event with confidence and focus, making the experience feel less daunting.

Another valuable strategy is to establish a time limit for your attendance. Knowing that you have permission to leave after a set period can alleviate anxiety. It can also provide a sense of control in a potentially chaotic environment. For instance, you might decide to stay for just one hour or until you've spoken to a few key people. This structure allows you to engage on your terms, helping to recharge your energy levels while still participating in the social scene.

Preparing conversation starters can also be a game changer. Introverts often feel more comfortable when they have a few topics in mind to discuss. Consider current events, shared interests, or even light-hearted questions that can spark engaging discussions. This preparation can reduce the pressure of thinking on your feet during the event, allowing you to focus on listening and connecting rather than feeling overwhelmed by the need to fill silences.

Finding a social buddy can significantly enhance your experience at gatherings. Partnering with a friend or acquaintance who understands your introverted nature can provide a support system. Having someone to share the experience with can make interactions feel less intimidating and more enjoyable. You can also rely on each other to take breaks when needed or to navigate conversations, creating a more comfortable atmosphere.

Finally, remember to prioritize self-care after attending social gatherings. Plan some downtime to recharge your batteries, whether through quiet reading, a nature walk, or engaging in a favorite hobby. Recognizing that social events can be draining allows you to take the necessary steps to recover and reflect on your experiences. Embracing these strategies and understanding your unique needs can transform social gatherings from daunting obligations into opportunities for connection and personal growth.

Leveraging Your Strengths in Teams

In a world that often seems to favor extroverted behaviors, introverts possess unique strengths that can be invaluable in team settings.

Understanding and leveraging these strengths can help introverts not only survive but thrive in collaborative environments. It's essential to recognize that the thoughtful, reflective nature of introverts often leads to deep insights and innovative ideas. By embracing this quality, introverts can contribute significantly to team discussions and decision-making processes, fostering a more inclusive atmosphere where diverse perspectives are valued.

One of the key strengths introverts bring to teams is their ability to listen actively. While some team members may dominate conversations, introverts excel at absorbing information, processing it, and providing considered feedback. This skill can create a balance in team dynamics, encouraging quieter voices to share their opinions. By positioning themselves as attentive listeners, introverts can facilitate open dialogues, ensuring everyone feels heard. This not only enhances team cohesion but also leads to more well-rounded solutions, as diverse viewpoints are integrated into the decision-making process.

Additionally, introverts often have a strong sense of focus and dedication. When working on tasks, they tend to dig deep and produce high-quality results. This intrinsic motivation can be a tremendous asset in team projects, where consistent effort and reliability are crucial. Introverts can leverage this strength by taking on roles that require concentration and attention to detail. By volunteering for tasks that align with their skills, introverts can not only shine individually but also elevate the overall performance of the team.

Moreover, introverts are often adept at problem-solving due to their reflective nature. They take the time to analyze situations thoroughly before jumping to conclusions, which can lead to creative solutions that others might overlook. In team settings, introverts can harness this analytical ability by proposing innovative ideas during brainstorming sessions or suggesting alternative approaches to challenges. By doing so, they can position themselves as valuable contributors and thought leaders, reinforcing their role within the team.

Lastly, it's vital for introverts to practice self-advocacy within their teams. They should feel empowered to communicate their strengths and preferences clearly, whether it's through one-on-

one conversations or team discussions. By articulating how they work best, introverts can create an environment that respects their need for social recharge while still allowing them to engage meaningfully with their colleagues. Embracing their unique qualities not only helps introverts succeed but also enriches the team experience as a whole, fostering a culture of appreciation for diverse working styles.

Finding Comfort in Group Dynamics

Finding comfort in group dynamics can seem daunting for introverts, but it holds the potential for growth and connection. When the hustle and bustle of daily life feels overwhelming, seeking solace in a supportive group can be a powerful antidote. Understanding that you are not alone in your experiences is the first step toward embracing group dynamics. Introverts often thrive in smaller, more intimate settings where they can engage meaningfully without the pressure of large crowds. Look for gatherings that prioritize deep conversations over superficial interactions, allowing you to recharge while connecting with others.

Establishing boundaries is essential for introverts in group settings. Recognize your limits and communicate them to those around you. Whether it's taking breaks when you feel drained or choosing not to engage in every conversation, honoring your needs will help you feel more comfortable. This proactive approach fosters an environment where you can contribute at your own pace, ensuring that you remain engaged without feeling overwhelmed. Remember, it's perfectly acceptable to step back and take a moment to breathe, allowing you to recharge and re-enter the group when you're ready.

Finding a group that aligns with your interests can significantly enhance your comfort level. Join clubs, workshops, or classes that focus on activities you enjoy. This common ground provides an excellent foundation for building connections without the pressure of forced socialization. When you share a passion with others, it creates an instant bond and makes conversation flow more naturally. Engaging with like-minded individuals can help alleviate social anxiety, making the experience more enjoyable and fulfilling.

Moreover, it's essential to recognize the value that each member brings to a group dynamic. Introverts often underestimate their contributions, but your unique perspective is a vital asset. Embrace your strengths, such as active listening and thoughtful insights, which can enrich conversations and deepen relationships. By valuing your role within the group, you can cultivate a sense of belonging that reinforces your confidence and encourages further participation. Celebrate the small victories as you engage more openly with others, knowing that your presence is meaningful.

Lastly, remember that group dynamics are not about changing who you are but finding a comfortable space to express yourself. Give yourself permission to explore different groups until you find one that resonates with you. The journey may involve some trial and error, but each experience is an opportunity for growth. Learning to navigate group settings can lead to enriching connections and a greater understanding of yourself. Embrace this journey with an open heart, knowing that finding comfort in group dynamics can be a rewarding aspect of your life as an introvert.

10

Embracing Change and Growth

Overcoming Fear of New Experiences

Fear of new experiences can often loom large for introverts, who may prefer the comfort of familiar routines and environments. However, stepping outside of these boundaries can lead to personal growth and fulfillment. Embracing new experiences does not mean extinguishing your introverted nature; rather, it can offer opportunities to expand your comfort zone while still honoring your need for solitude and reflection. Recognizing that fear is a natural response can help you navigate the anxiety that often accompanies trying something new.

To overcome the fear of new experiences, start by reframing your mindset. Instead of viewing new situations as potential threats, consider them as opportunities for learning and growth. This shift in perspective allows you to approach new activities with curiosity rather than apprehension. Remind yourself that every new experience has the potential to teach you something valuable, whether it's a new skill, a new perspective, or simply a new way of connecting with others. By focusing on the positives, you can reduce anxiety and open yourself up to the possibilities that await.

Setting small, manageable goals can also be an effective strategy for introverts looking to embrace new experiences. Rather than diving headfirst into a large, overwhelming event, start with something small. Attend a local workshop, join a book club, or participate in a community event. These smaller steps can help you build confidence and gradually acclimate to new situations. Celebrate your successes, no matter how minor they may seem. Each small victory reinforces your ability to handle new experiences and can serve as motivation to take on bigger challenges in the future.

Finding a supportive network can make a significant difference in overcoming fear. Surround yourself with friends or fellow introverts who encourage you to step outside your comfort zone. Sharing your fears and aspirations with others can alleviate feelings of isolation and provide you with a sense of camaraderie. You might even find that others share similar fears, creating an environment where you can support one another in exploring new experiences together. This shared journey can transform daunting challenges into exciting adventures.

Lastly, practice self-compassion throughout this journey. Understand that it's normal to feel nervous or hesitant when facing new experiences. Allow yourself the grace to feel these emotions without judgment, and remember that it's okay to take a step back if needed. Prioritize self-care and recharge after each new experience, giving yourself the time and space to reflect on what you've learned. By approaching new experiences with patience and kindness towards yourself, you'll cultivate a more resilient mindset and empower yourself to continue exploring the world around you.

Setting Personal Goals

Setting personal goals is an essential step for introverts seeking to navigate the complexities of a busy life while honoring their unique needs and strengths. As an introvert, it is crucial to establish objectives that reflect your values and aspirations, allowing you to create a fulfilling and balanced life. By taking the time to identify specific goals, you can channel your energy toward what truly matters, ensuring that you remain engaged and motivated in both personal and professional realms.

Begin by reflecting on what areas of your life need the most attention. Consider aspects such as career, relationships, self-care, or hobbies. This introspection is vital for introverts, as it allows you to tap into your inner thoughts and feelings.

Write down your ideas, prioritizing goals that resonate deeply with you. Focus on quality over quantity; having a few meaningful goals can be more impactful than a long list of vague aspirations. Remember, the journey toward achieving these goals is just as important as the goals themselves.

Once you have a clear understanding of your priorities, break your goals down into manageable steps. This approach not only makes your objectives feel less daunting but also allows you to celebrate small victories along the way. Introverts often thrive in structured environments, so creating a timeline for each goal can help you stay organized and accountable. By setting realistic deadlines, you give yourself the grace to work at your own pace while still making progress.

Incorporating self-care practices into your goal-setting strategy is vital for maintaining balance. As an introvert, you may find that social interactions can drain your energy, making it essential to schedule regular downtime. Designate specific times for recharging, whether through solitary activities like reading, meditation, or enjoying nature. These moments of reflection will not only help you rejuvenate but will also enhance your focus and motivation as you work toward your goals.

Lastly, remain flexible and open to adjusting your goals as needed. Life is unpredictable, and introverts may find themselves feeling overwhelmed at times. Embrace the idea that it is perfectly acceptable to reassess your objectives and modify them to better fit your evolving needs. By allowing yourself the freedom to adapt, you can cultivate a more positive and resilient mindset. Remember, setting personal goals is a journey of self-discovery and growth, and with each step, you are one step closer to achieving the balance you seek in your life.

Celebrating Your Progress

Celebrating your progress as an introvert is essential for maintaining motivation and a positive mindset amidst the demands of a busy life. Often, introverts find themselves caught in the whirlwind of responsibilities and social obligations, which can overshadow their achievements. Acknowledging your growth, no matter how small, can provide a much-needed boost to your self-esteem and reinforce your commitment to personal development. Every step you take, from managing your time more effectively to mastering social recharge techniques, deserves recognition and celebration.

To effectively celebrate your progress, consider keeping a journal dedicated to your achievements and reflections. This space allows you to document milestones, whether it's successfully navigating a challenging social situation or implementing a new time management strategy. Writing down your thoughts not only helps you to see how far you've come but also provides a tangible reminder of your capabilities. On days when you feel overwhelmed, revisiting your journal can serve as a source of encouragement, reminding you of your resilience and resourcefulness.

In addition to journaling, sharing your accomplishments with a trusted friend or family member can amplify the celebration. As introverts, we may be inclined to downplay our successes, but expressing them to someone who understands and supports you can enhance the experience. This exchange can create a supportive atmosphere where you can both celebrate progress and provide encouragement to one another. Engaging in these conversations not only reinforces your achievements but also fosters deeper connections, which can be uplifting in a busy world.

Incorporating small rewards into your routine can also make the celebration of progress more meaningful. After completing a challenging task or reaching a personal goal, treat yourself to something that brings you joy—this could be a quiet evening with a good book, a favorite snack, or a short retreat into nature. These moments of self-care not only acknowledge your hard work but also provide essential recharging time, allowing you to maintain your balance in the face of a hectic schedule.

Ultimately, celebrating your progress is about recognizing the unique journey of being an introvert in a busy world. Each accomplishment, whether large or small, contributes to your overall growth and well-being. By consciously making the effort to honor your achievements, you cultivate a greater appreciation for your strengths and capabilities. This practice will empower you to continue navigating life's challenges with confidence, ensuring that you thrive rather than merely survive in your daily pursuits.

11

Conclusion: Your Journey as an Introvert

Reflecting on Your Growth

Reflecting on your growth is an essential practice for introverts navigating the complexities of a busy life. It allows you to take a step back and appreciate the progress you've made, no matter how small. As introverts, we often focus on the challenges we face, whether it's managing time effectively or finding space for social recharge. By consciously reflecting on your growth, you can cultivate a deeper understanding of your strengths, acknowledge your achievements, and foster a positive mindset that propels you forward.

Begin by creating a safe space for reflection. This could be as simple as a quiet corner in your home or a favorite café where you feel comfortable. Set aside dedicated time to gather your thoughts and consider the experiences you've had over the past months or even years. Ask yourself guiding questions: What challenges have I overcome? How have I managed my time in ways that honor my introverted nature? What social situations have I navigated successfully? Answering these questions can unveil insights that contribute to your growth narrative.

Next, celebrate your milestones, both big and small. Introverts often downplay their achievements, feeling that they do not measure up to more extroverted standards. However, every step you take toward finding your balance is worthy of recognition. Perhaps you successfully attended a social gathering that once felt overwhelming, or you implemented a time management strategy that allowed you to reclaim precious downtime. Acknowledging these victories reinforces your resilience and encourages you to continue striving for balance.

As you reflect, consider the lessons learned from experiences that didn't go as planned. Analyzing what went wrong and how you felt can provide valuable insights into your preferences and needs. Did a particular situation drain your energy? Did you feel rushed or overwhelmed? By understanding these feelings, you can better prepare for similar scenarios in the future. This knowledge empowers you to set boundaries and prioritize your well-being, ensuring that you remain proactive in managing your busy life.

Finally, incorporate your reflections into actionable strategies for the future. Use the insights you've gained to create a personalized plan that aligns with your introverted nature. Set achievable goals that respect your need for solitude while also encouraging you to step out of your comfort zone when necessary. This balanced approach allows you to embrace growth without losing sight of what makes you uniquely you. Remember, the journey of self-discovery is ongoing, and each moment of reflection brings you closer to the balanced life you aspire to lead.

Continuing the Conversation

Continuing the conversation is essential for introverts navigating a busy life. While social interactions can often feel draining, engaging in meaningful dialogue can lead to deeper connections and a greater sense of community. As you strive to balance your introverted nature with the demands of daily life, remember that every conversation is an opportunity to share your thoughts, learn from others, and cultivate relationships that nourish your spirit. Embrace the idea that your voice matters, and take small steps to keep the dialogue flowing without overwhelming yourself.

One effective strategy to continue conversations is to set clear intentions before social gatherings. Think about what you want to achieve from the interaction. Whether it's reconnecting with an old friend or getting to know a colleague better, having a purpose can help you feel more grounded. Additionally, preparing a few open-ended questions can ease the pressure of thinking on the spot. Questions like, "What has been the highlight of your week?" or "What projects are you currently passionate about?" can stimulate engaging discussions and take the focus off you, allowing the conversation to unfold naturally.

Another valuable technique is to practice active listening. This involves not just hearing the words spoken but truly engaging with them. By focusing on the speaker and responding thoughtfully, you can foster a more meaningful exchange. Reflecting back what you've heard or asking follow-up questions demonstrates your genuine interest and encourages the other person to open up further. This approach not only helps maintain the conversation but also allows you to recharge socially without the pressure of having to dominate the dialogue.

It's also important to recognize when to take breaks during social interactions. Introverts often need moments of solitude to recharge, especially in large or prolonged gatherings. Don't hesitate to step away for a few minutes, whether it's to grab a drink, take a breath of fresh air, or simply find a quiet corner. These brief intermissions will help you maintain your energy levels, ensuring that you can engage more meaningfully when you return to the conversation. Remember, it's perfectly acceptable to prioritize your well-being while still being present for those around you.

Lastly, consider following up after conversations. A simple text or email expressing your enjoyment of the discussion can leave a lasting impression and keep the connection alive. Sharing an article, a resource, or even a funny anecdote related to your conversation can spark further dialogue. This not only helps you maintain relationships but also allows you to express your thoughts in a way that feels comfortable for you. Continuing the conversation doesn't stop at the event; it can be a dynamic process that enriches your life and fosters a supportive network of friends and colleagues.

Encouragement for the Future

As you navigate the complexities of a busy life, it's essential to remember that your introverted nature is not a limitation but a unique strength. Embracing who you are allows you to harness your deep thinking and reflective qualities, which can lead to innovative solutions in both your personal and professional life. The world values diverse perspectives, and your ability to observe and analyze situations can help you stand out in any crowded room. Recognizing this can serve as a powerful motivator, encouraging you to pursue your goals with confidence.

Time management is crucial for maintaining balance in your life. As an introvert, you may find that your energy levels fluctuate based on your environment and interactions. Prioritize tasks that align with your natural rhythms, tackling challenging work during your peak productivity hours and reserving time for recharge afterward. Consider using tools like planners or digital apps that suit your style, allowing you to map out your days in a way that feels comfortable yet productive. By mastering time management, you create a sense of control that can alleviate feelings of overwhelm.

Social situations can often feel draining, but remember that you have the power to design your social experiences. Choose environments and gatherings that resonate with you, and don't hesitate to set boundaries that protect your energy. Whether it's engaging in smaller gatherings or scheduling breaks during larger events, you can craft social interactions that feel rewarding rather than exhausting. This approach will not only enhance your enjoyment of socializing but also empower you to build meaningful connections at your own pace.

As you look to the future, consider the importance of self-compassion. It's easy to fall into the trap of comparing yourself to more extroverted peers, but each personality type brings value to the table. Celebrate your achievements, no matter how small, and recognize that every step you take contributes to your growth. Keep a journal or a record of your successes to remind yourself of your progress and resilience. This practice can serve as a source of motivation during challenging times, reinforcing the idea that your journey is uniquely yours.

Finally, envision a future where you thrive as the introvert you are. Picture yourself engaging with the world in ways that feel authentic and fulfilling. With every strategy you implement, you are crafting a life that honors your introverted tendencies while allowing for growth and connection. The path may not always be easy, but by embracing your individuality and prioritizing your well-being, you can create a balanced life that not only sustains you but also inspires others. Your journey is just beginning, and the future holds endless possibilities for you to explore.

Milton Keynes UK
Ingram Content Group UK Ltd.
UKHW031456061124
450821UK00004B/336